WORLDVIEW GUIDE

FRANKENSTEIN

Jake McAtee

canonpress
Moscow, Idaho

Published by Canon Press
P.O. Box 8729, Moscow, Idaho 83843
800.488.2034 | www.canonpress.com

Jake McAtee, *Worldview Guide for Frankenstein*
Copyright ©2020 by Jake McAtee.
Cited page numbers come from the Canon Classics edition of the book, www.
canonpress.com/books/canon-classics.

Cover design by James Engerbretson
Cover illustration by Forrest Dickison
Interior design by Valerie Anne Bost and James Engerbretson

Printed in the United States of America.

Library of Congress Cataloging-in-Publication Data forthcoming

A free end-of-book test and answer key are available for download at
www.canonpress.com/ClassicsQuizzes

20 21 22 23 24 25   9 8 7 6 5 4 3 2 1

CONTENTS

INTRODUCTION

Young Victor Frankenstein leaves his family to attend University with dreams of curing humanity from illnesses like the one that overcame his mother. Possessed by the thrill of uncovering nature's secrets, Victor discovers the *élan vitale*, the secret to generating life. His ambition drives him into a sickly obsession for the next year, rifling through graveyards, carefully crafting a new humanity, an Adam to a new human race—one that would call him their god.

And it works.

Before him, prostrate on a table, lies the fruit of his terrible labor. Everything has gone to plan. That is, until the creature opens his eyes....

THE WORLD AROUND

Any teacher worth their salt will tell you history is complicated, and nothing gives a better picture of that fact like the world around Mary Shelley's life.

The late 18th century was a time of *Revolution!* and Mary's parents were in the middle of it all in England. Across the Atlantic Sea, the American Revolution's first shot rang out in 1775. Shortly after the end of that war, tensions in France came to a head in the storming of the Bastille. The French Revolution quickly turned into a vicious cycle of bloodletting on the guillotine.

It was in Paris during the Revolution that one journalist, crossing the square in the hunt for her story, slipped and fell in a puddle. She was horrified when she realized that it hadn't been rain or water tossed to clean the street, but a pool of blood. This journalist was Mary Wollstonecraft, the mother of Mary Shelley. Mary Wollstonecraft would contribute much to the intellectual air of the time, and is considered by many to be the first feminist. Despite her horror of slipping in a pool of blood, Wollstonecraft would rebut Edmond Burke's *Reflections on the Revolution in France*, which criticized the whole affair, by writing *A Vindication of the Rights of Man*, published anonymously. Years later she would pen *A Vindication of the Rights of Women*.

After the last head rolled, Wollstonecraft would settle down with another radical, William Godwin. Godwin's work on political justice and anarchy fueled revolutionary fires and earned him several revolutionary friends. Mary and William's social circle featured several American notables such as Thomas Paine and Benjamin Franklin. The couple even helped Aaron Burr when he fell on hard times. One friendship of Godwin's that would prove to have a lasting effect on his daughter Mary was the romantic poet Samuel Taylor Coleridge.

But it wasn't all violence: America experienced the growing pains of major expansion across the frontier with the Louisiana Purchase in 1803.

In France, decades of turmoil came to an end as Napoleon abdicated the throne in 1814.

All of this is the backdrop against which Mary Shelley would publish her debut novel, *Frankenstein, or the Modern Prometheus*, in 1818.

While a broad lens may indicate that this was a time of bad actors in the political and literary world, it wasn't all politically radical and immoral. Providence did not leave us without any literary edification: It was at this time that

Jane Austen was writing her novels: *Pride and Prejudice* was published in 1813 and *Emma* in 1815.

ABOUT THE AUTHOR

Mary Shelley's life was a deeply unhappy one. Like her work, it was marked by extreme, untethered passion and turmoil. She was born August 30th, 1797 to social radicals Mary Wollstonecraft and William Godwin. Her mother died eleven days later due to complications with her delivery. Mary was received by her older sister Fanny (from a previous relationship her mother had had with a soldier), and a little sister Claire would be added less than a year later, after William Godwin's remarriage.

Percy Bysshe Shelley, a married man and disciple of her father's anarchical works, wrote to Godwin about his great influence on his life. Godwin was used to passionate young men eager to apprentice under him, but when Percy made it clear he would like to become a patron, Godwin's posture towards the stranger became very open. In his letters, Godwin would tell Shelley that he and the girls were eager to know more about his past and passions. It

wouldn't be long before Shelley was hailed as a romantic hero by everyone in the house.[1]

Percy eventually left his pregnant wife to stay with Godwin and his family. He would tutor Godwin's kids and continue to help pay Godwin's bills. It wasn't long before Percy became romantically interested in Mary, and eventually, to her father's great regret, Mary left home with Percy and her stepsister Claire. Godwin, a proponent of revolutionizing the moral order and in particular sexual norms, had made his intellectual bed and found it very uncomfortable.

Percy's abandoned wife would eventually commit suicide.

In 1816, Mary gave birth to a baby girl who died a few days later. That summer, Percy, Mary, and her younger sister Claire joined the notorious poet Lord Byron and writer John Polidori at a cabin where *Frankenstein* was born. It was shortly after this that Mary's sister Fanny committed suicide back in England. *Frankenstein* was published anonymously two years later, leading to the belief that Percy might have written it.

Over the next few years, the Shelleys lost two more children, and, at the age of twenty-four, Mary was left a widow when Percy Shelley drowned while sailing with a friend off the coast of Spain. Mary would go on to write four more books, *Valperga* (1823), *The Last Man* (1826), the autobiographical *Lodore* (1835), and lastly *Mathilde*, published after her death at the age of 53 due to brain cancer.

---

1. Miranda Seymour, *Mary Shelley* (London: Simon & Schuster, 2000), 68.

WHAT OTHER NOTABLES SAID

"The author [of *Frankenstein*] has powers, both of conception and language, which employed in a happier direction might, perhaps, (we speak dubiously,) give him a name among these whose writings amuse or amend their fellow-creatures; but we take the liberty of assuring him, and hope that he may be in a temper to listen to us, that the style which he has adopted in the present publication merely tends to defeat his own purpose, if he really had any other object in view than that of leaving the wearied reader, after a struggle between laughter and loathing, in doubt whether the head or the heart of the author be the most diseased."[2] - *Quarterly Review* in 1818

"There never was a wilder story imagined, yet, like most of the fictions of this age, it has an air of reality attached to it, by being connected with the favourite

---

2. John Wilson Croker, *Quarterly Review* 18 (January [delayed until 12 June] 1818): 379-85.

projects and passions of the times."[3] ~ *The Edinburgh Magazine*

"The novel of *Frankenstein* is undoubtedly, as a mere story, one of the most original and complete productions of the day." ~ Percy Bysshe Shelley

"A tissue of horrible and disgusting absurdity...the dreams of insanity are embodied in the strong and striking language of the insane, and the author...often leaves us in doubt whether he is not as mad as his hero." ~ *Quarterly Review*, 1818

---

3. *The Edinburgh Magazine and Literary Miscellany*, A New Series of "The Scots Magazine" 2 (March 1818): 249-53.

SETTING, CHARACTERS, AND PLOT SUMMARY (600 WORDS)

Setting:

Frankenstein begins and ends in the Arctic Ocean. The plot is mainly centered in Switzerland.

Main Characters:

• **Robert Walton:** An explorer on an expedition in the Arctic tundra. His are the first and last words of the novel in his letters to his sister Margaret. He rescues Victor, who, after learning more about his rescuer, discloses his marvelous cautionary tale.

• **Victor Frankenstein:** Victor is the creator of the monster

• **The Monster:** Victor's regrettable creation, *not* named Frankenstein, despite modern confusion.

• **Elizabeth Lavenza:** Victor's bride

• **William Frankenstein:** Victor's little brother

• **Alphonse Frankenstein:** Victor's father

• **Henry Clerval:** Victor's best friend

• **Justine Moritz:** The nanny / housekeeper accused of murdering Victor's brother, William

Plot

Frankenstein is bookended by the letters of Robert Walton to his sister Margaret. Robert is an explorer on an expedition in the Arctic tundra. He rescues the protagonist, Victor Frankenstein, from the tundra and sustains him for a time. Upon hearing Robert's dreams and aspirations for glory, Victor hopes to warn him by offering his horrifying testimony.

After his mother's death, Victor Frankenstein heads to school to study the sciences. He has dreams of curing human afflictions and becoming like a god to humanity. He leaves his fiancée and his family to get his education at the University of Ingolstadt.

Once he discovers that he can galvanize life, he works himself sick. At school Victor becomes obsessed. He's not eating. His family hardly ever hears from him and his friends hardly see him. Only upon completion, once his creation opens its eyes, do the consequences of his actions become clear to him. He flees in terror to his friend Henry's home, where he tries to recover from years of sickness and guilt.

During his stay, Victor receives a letter to come home from his father. His brother William has been strangled to death. The housekeeper and nanny, Justine, has been accused of the crime. But Victor knows she has been wrongly accused. His guilt tells him exactly who the murderer is—his Monster.

At home, his guilt weighs heavier. Despite knowing deep in his bones who murdered his brother, he cannot bring himself to tell anyone. Not his father or his fiancée. Not even Justine, condemned to die for something she didn't do. Unable to cope, he flees to Geneva in hopes of some relief from his guilt.

In Geneva, the Monster reveals himself to Victor and they ascend to a hut in the mountains. It's here that the Monster tells Victor what he's been up to. He has taught himself to speak and to read via a family in the woods. He has also learned of his creation through a notebook Victor had left. He tells Victor about his attempt to reveal himself to the family who has taught him so much, but they rejected him on sight. In the aftermath of another rejection, he confesses that he took his anger out on Victor's family, and strangled William.

The Monster requests that Victor make him a wife and promises they would flee to another continent, never to be heard from again. He only wants someone to be with. Victor at first agrees, but unable to bear the growing weight of creating a race of monsters, destroys the Monster's bride halfway through. Rejected again, the Monster vows destruction on the life of his creator. Victor flees to Ireland.

Shortly after his arrival, the body of Henry Clerval, Victor's best friend, is found on the shore, and Victor is nearly convicted of the murder. Once deemed innocent, Victor hopes to restore his happiness by marrying the love of his life, Elizabeth. This is just the moment when the Monster makes good on his promise to be with him *always*, even on his wedding night.

After the murder of Elizabeth, the Monster flees. Victor, without anything else to live for, gives chase. He hunts him around Europe and up through Russia, eventually finding Robert Walton's ship in the Arctic.

Victor dies shortly after disclosing his story. The night of Victor's death, Robert happens upon the Monster crouching over Victor in inconsolable grief. The Monster offers his regret and remorse to Robert, and then departs toward his promised funeral pyre.

QUOTABLES

"I saw—with shut eyes, but acute mental vision—I saw the pale student of unhallowed arts kneeling beside the thing he had put together. I saw the hideous phantasm of a man stretched out, and then, on the working of some powerful engine, show signs of life and stir with an uneasy, half-vital motion. Frightful must it be, for supremely frightful would be the effect of any human endeavor to mock the stupendous mechanism of the Creator of the world." *~Author's introduction of original*, p. xxix[4]

"It was the secrets of heaven and earth that I desired to learn; and whether it was the outward substance of things or the inner spirit of nature and the mysterious soul of man that occupied me, still my inquiries were directed to the metaphysical, or in its highest sense, the physical secrets of the world." ~Victor Frankenstein, Chapter 2, p. 25

---

4. All page numbers are taken from the Canon Classics edition.

"One man's life or death were but a small price to pay for the acquirement of the knowledge which I sought, for the dominion I should acquire and transmit over the elemental foes of our race." ~Robert Walton, Letter 4, p. 15

"In other studies you go as far as others have gone before you, and there is nothing more to know; but in a scientific pursuit there is continual food for discovery and wonder." ~Victor Frankenstein, Chapter 4, p. 40

"Alas! Victor, when falsehood can look so like the truth, who can assure themselves of certain happiness?" ~Elizabeth, Chapter 9, p. 83

"He had come forth from the hands of God a perfect creature, happy and prosperous, guarded by the special care of his Creator; he was allowed to converse with and acquire knowledge from beings of a superior nature, but I was wretched, helpless, and alone." ~The Monster, Chapter 15, p. 122

"Cursed, cursed creator! Why did I live? Why, in that instant, did I not extinguish the spark of existence which you had so wantonly bestowed? I know not; despair had not yet taken possession of me; my feelings were those of rage and revenge. I could with pleasure have destroyed the cottage and its inhabitants and have glutted myself with their shrieks and misery." ~The Monster, Chapter 16, p. 129

WORLDVIEW ANALYSIS

Frankenstein, the genesis of the horror genre, began with friends gathered around a campfire telling ghost stories. For a modern generation raised on *Goosebumps* it's a little too good to be true.

The promiscuous crew trying to scare one another senseless consisted of a *who's-who* of the literary scene at the time: Lord Byron, Percy Bysshe Shelley, John Polidori, Mary Godwin, and her little sister Claire. Little did they know, the story Mary told that night would far outlive its author.

Two hundred years after publication, Mary's story hasn't slowed a bit. In the introduction to the latest illustrated edition of *Frankenstein*, famous director Guillermo Del Toro says that *Frankenstein* provided his "road to Damascus" moment:

> It illuminated the reason I loved monsters, my kinship with them, and showed me how deep, how life-changing a monster parable could be—how it could function as art and how it could reach across

17

distance and time and become a palliative to solitude and pain.[5]

He continues that every time we read her novel,

> . . . we try, in return, to help (Mary's) creature stay alive. We strive to turn a curse into a blessing . . . We hope that in some way, somehow, our gratitude, our love, can reach him like a whispered prayer, like a distant song. And we dream that perhaps he can stop—amid the frozen tundra and the screaming wind—and turn his head and look back. At us. And we hope that then he might recognize in our eyes his own yearning. And that perchance we can walk toward each other and find meager warmth in our embrace. And then, if only for a moment, we will not feel alone in the world.[6]

Del Toro and critics like him illustrate how often *Frankenstein* is misread, construing the monster into a mistreated and misunderstood minority. If only Victor and the other characters had exhibited any hospitality or empathy or at the very least provided him a wife, then maybe he'd have been as well adjusted as any person we might know. One only wonders if Del Toro had been there to open the mead hall door and offer that stray pup Grendel a seat with the rest of them with his own cup of mead, *Beowulf* would read differently too.

---

5. *The New Annotated Frankenstein*, ed. Leslie S. Klinger (New York: W.W. Norton, 2017), xvi.

6. Ibid., xvi-xvii.

In *Frankenstein*, Mary Shelley was making a point about the frightening judgment of cumulative transgressions, not offering a reductio on the sins of inhospitality. Perhaps sexual freedom doesn't end in liberty of consciousness, but of never-ending guilt. *Frankenstein* subtitled, *The Modern Promestheus*, is a story about the horror of your past growing legs and catching up to you, not about the radicalization of the lonely.

Passion Unbound

Unlike her husband Percy and her biological parents, Mary was beginning to grow uncertain of the radicalism around her. Remember that Mary was the child of two radical revolutionaries. Both her parents (Mary Wollstonecraft and William Godwin) contributed to the literature and academic spirit of the enlightenment that sought to throw off Europe's Christian inheritance. They were both proponents of the French Revolution and utilized their own revolutionary treatises to keep that fire burning.

A central tenant of their musings was that they viewed constraints of any passion to be a form of slavery. Nowhere is this clearer than (of course) sexual passions. Percy Shelley in his prose notes to his poem Queen Mab[7] parroted a sentiment learned from Mary and William Godwin:

"Love withers under constraint: its very essence is liberty.... How long then ought the sexual connection to last...?

---

7. A poem ironically dedicated to his wife Harriet: "Thou wert the inspiration of my song."

A husband and wife ought to continue so long united as they love each other: any law which should bind them to cohabitation for one moment after the decay of their affection, would be a most intolerable tyranny, and the most unworthy of toleration."[8] Additionally, he wrote, "A system could not well have been devised more studiously hostile to human happiness than marriage."[9] Godwin and the rest were convinced that applying boundary lines and limits on their passions was wholly unnatural, put in place by tyrannical traditionalists.

G.K. Chesterton once said that,

> There exists in such a case a certain institution or law; let us say, for the sake of simplicity, a fence or gate erected across a road. The more modern type of reformer goes gaily up to it and says, 'I don't see the use of this; let us clear it away.' To which the more intelligent type of reformer will do well to answer: 'If you don't see the use of it, I certainly won't let you clear it away. Go away and think. Then, when you can come back and tell me that you do see the use of it, I may allow you to destroy it.'[10]

The revolutionaries were the impatient folks, eager to toss Chesterton's fence without asking why it had been put there in the first place. They were convinced, along with Rousseau that mankind was free but everywhere in

8. Shelley, *The Poems of Shelley: Volume One: 1804-1817* (1989; New York: Routledge, 2014), 368, lines 40-48.

9. Ibid., 372-73.

10. *The Thing* (1929; London: Sheed and Ward, 1946), 29.

chains. Of course, this didn't prohibit any of our cast of characters from having marriages—just not happy and durable marriages.

In this regard, Percy Shelley was an excellent and thorough student of Godwin. He confidently walked in light of this teaching without blushing once. He, with no regard to his marriage, would eventually seduce William Godwin's daughter Mary under the guise of his tutelage. William Godwin was not happy about this, but what could he do? Godwin's bill were still being paid by Percy and his own disdain of any sexual norms could be found at the nearest book store. He watched his ideas enfleshed in the person of Percy Shelley—running away with both of his teenage daughters. Stuck between the rock of a father's love for his daughter and the hard place of needing Percy's money, he caved and continued to receive Percy's money.

No one in this group recanted any of their revolutionary ideals, but Mary Shelley would, at the very least, become skeptical. The (short) life she lived alongside her husband Percy left a violent wake of harm and destruction.

In contrast to her peers and parents, it's clear from *Frankenstein* that Mary grew skeptical of the idea that transgressing the limits and boundaries of our desires led to freedom. Instead of freedom, she would come to believe instead that these sins accumulate and consume our lives and taint the lives of those close to them. The sins of the past, when harbored and nursed, are like a festering

wound. Guilt haunts, stalking us and everything we put
our hand to do.

In *Frankenstein*, Mary Shelley proposes a world where
these transgressions are committed and there is only the
monster of remorse and retribution. In the world of *Frankenstein*, and in the world of its author, there is no remis-
sion of sins—there is no forgiveness.

Percy Shelley's Prometheus

There is some debate about who *really* wrote *Frankenstein:
The Modern Prometheus.* At publication, and for a time after, it was published anonymously. Percy is given credit for
portions and even the totality of the work. But if there's
one thing we know, it couldn't have been Percy, and the
reason is important to my argument here. Percy could not
have written it because the story is critical of mankind's
capacity to achieve utopian world by means of revolution
of the moral order. *Frankenstein* was Percy's literary biog-
raphy of sorts—written by his wife, who was able to see
more clearly than he did. The evidence of this can be seen
in the couple's differing takes on the myth of Prometheus.
In the Grecian tale, the Titan Prometheus takes from the
god Zeus what isn't his. He steals fire from Mount Olym-
pus and offers it to humanity. Zeus punishes this immor-
tal being by chaining him to a rock and every day having
his regenerative liver eaten by an eagle.

In his four act poem "Prometheus Unbound," Percy Bysshe Shelley retells the myth, having Prometheus

escape from punishment with the help of Hercules. By the end, the tyrant Jupiter has fallen and mankind is finally free. Not only is mankind free, but in their freedom humanity evolved:

> but man
> Equal, unclassed, tribeless, and nationless,
> Exempt from awe, worship, degree, the king
> Over himself; just, gentle, wise; but man
> Passionless—no, yet free from guilt or pain,
> Act III: 194-99

In this revolution, man has evolved and become *more* human. They are not passionless robots—they have moved beyond the negative consequences of passion: *Passionless—no, yet free from guilt or pain*. Man free from the tyrants of gods has become the Übermensch in Dostoevsky's *Crime and Punishment*, "beyond" guilt or pain, a Napoleon, a god:

> The lightning is his slave; heaven's utmost deep
> Gives up her stars, and like a flock of sheep
> They pass before his eye, are numbered, and roll on!
> The tempest is his steed, he strides the air;
> And the abyss shouts from her depth laid bare,
> 'Heaven, hast thou secrets? Man unveils me; I have none.'
> Act IV: 418-23

Man, out from under the bondage and lies of class, nation, awe, and worship, now owns the heavens and uncovers the secrets of the abyss. Knowledge has saved humanity.

Here we connect to Mary's story: The possession of *this* knowledge, the "secrets of heaven and earth," as Victor Frankenstein puts it (25), is precisely the motivation not only of Frankenstein, but of Robert Walton, the explorer who bookends Mary's novel.[11] How does Mary's "modern" tale compare with her husband's?

Mary Shelley's "Modern Prometheus"

At the beginning of Mary's novel, her main character has all of the same hopes and dreams that rhyme with Percy's "Prometheus Unbound." Victor Frankenstein begins his tale of sorrow by telling us what he's like in contrast with his love, Elizabeth. She, like the ideal Romantic heroine, busied herself with the sublime and the poets. But Victor, on the other hand, was obsessed with knowledge. "The world was to me a secret which I desired to divine. Curiosity, earnest research to learn the hidden laws of nature, gladness akin to rapture, as they were unfolded to me, are among the earliest sensations I can remember"(24).

Victor took up the study of science. He was aware of the modern arts of science and their father Sir Isaac Newton, heroes of the Enlightenment thinkers. But there was another line of "scientists," disregarded by the moderns of the day (especially his father). These were authors such as Cornelius Agrippa, Paracelsus, and Albertus Magnus. "I read and studied the wild fancies of these writers with

---

11. See the *Quotables* section of this Worldview Guide for Walton and Frankenstein's complete quotes about this secret knowledge.

delight..." (27). The books tapped into the "unknowable" by modern means, discerning things that couldn't be discovered beneath a microscope. And his "dreams were therefore undisturbed by scientific reality." Mary's Prometheus, Victor Frankenstein, seems to have his own copy of Percy's poem: "what glory would attend the discovery, if I could banish disease from the human frame" (28). "A new species would bless me as its creator and source...no father could claim the gratitude of his child so completely as I should deserve theirs" (43).

At university, Victor happens upon the secret to generating life, and his obsession drives him to illness. Undistracted by the obviously debilitating obsession, he completes his project and sends electricity through his corpse, bringing the creature to life.

And here, Mary's vision breaks from her husband's. You can surely imagine, were Percy writing, the vaulted prose describing the new creation as a cornerstone to his New World. Humanity is saved, free from bondage to tradition! But instead, Mary's Prometheus begins his descent into a horrifying tragedy. As the creature opens his eyes, Victor's reality comes into terrifying clarity. Regret courses through Victor as he sees the hideous fruit he's born. He flees in shame and terror.

Victor Frankenstein has planted the virtues of the romantic period, with its utopian vision fueled by alchemy and science and untethered passion. But he has reaped a terrible harvest. *The Modern Prometheus* is not *Prometheus Unbound*.

The Daemon, Remorse & Retribution

After the death of William Frankenstein and Justine, Victor waxes eloquent about the need for a change of scenery: "I suddenly left my home, and bending my steps towards the near Alpine valleys, sought in the magnificence, the eternity of such scenes, to forget myself and my ephemeral, because human, sorrows"(84). There, the Monster reveals himself to Victor and they discuss what happened that night and what has happened since. It's here that we first get to hear from the Monster.

On the mountain, the *daemon*, as Victor will refer to him, tells him he wishes to live a life inspired by all romantic impulses he's learned and developed. He's watched a poor family in a cottage in the woods for some time and has learned much. This is not the monster with his arms out and grunting that our culture has told us about. He's read books and feels the weight of his rejection and loneliness. In his reading of Milton's *Paradise Lost*, he identifies not with God's creation of Adam, but with the spurned creature Satan. He's filled with envy at the mere thought of his creator. *How dare you sport thus with life!* cries the Monster (90).

E. Michael Jones rightly describes the monster as retribution and "the reestablishment of moral equilibrium."[12] He is the ghost of victims wronged, "Remorse

---

12. E. Michael Jones, *Monsters from the Id: the Rise of Horror in Fiction and Film* (Dallas, TX: Spence Pub. Co., 2000), 85.

personified,"[13] a justification of wrong doings, the arm of natural law. It's as if you can hear the voice of the monster in Mary and Percy's victims as they condemn the pair for living as if there were no consequences. "Sporting with life" is a charge we could expect from Percy's first wife who committed suicide as her husband gallivanted around Europe with an underage Mary Shelley and her sister. It's what Fanny, the sister Mary and Claire left behind, and who also committed suicide, might say.

Victor and the Monster come to a short agreement on the mountain that a Bride will be created to satiate the Monster's loneliness. Several weeks in, Victor aborts the project, terrified of the consequences that would be reaped from creating a monstrous race.

After yet another rejection, the Monster vows to take from his Creator everyone he loves. Henry Clerval's dead body floats to the shore in Ireland and Victor is nearly indicted for the death. Afterwards Victor heads home to his last hope of starting anew, to marry his love Elizabeth. The monster however, makes good on his promise to be there on his wedding night, and he kills Elizabeth.

From here, the narrative oscillates between regret and hatred until at last everyone is dead. Indeed, even the monster, after his Creator dies, loses purpose. On Victor's death bed, the monster confesses to Robert more about himself and his motives. He is no abstract villain, created in a vacuum. He is instead a giant, hulking mass of

---

13. Ibid., 84.

graveyard flesh, made in the emotional image of his creator. From his "birth," even after his rejection, he is bound to his creator, and his hatred of his creator is at the center of everything he does. He's obsessed:

> After the murder of Clerval I returned to Switzerland, heart-broken and overcome. I pitied Frankenstein; my pity amounted to horror; I abhorred myself. But when I discovered that he, the author at once of my existence and of its unspeakable torments, dared to hope for happiness, that while he accumulated wretchedness and despair upon me he sought his own enjoyment in feelings and passions from the indulgence of which I was forever barred, then impotent envy and bitter indignation filled me with an insatiable thirst for vengeance. (216-17)

The monster describes a kaleidoscope of envy and hatred. His creator's existence has conflated with his own, he oscillates between pity and horror, hatred for his creator and hatred for himself. Love and life itself has become an object that cannot be shared by both of them. And if the monster is barred from either, then he will make sure his creator is barred as well.

> I recollected my threat and resolved that it should be accomplished. I knew that I was preparing for myself a deadly torture, but I was the slave, not the master, of an impulse which I detested yet could not disobey. Yet when she died! Nay, then I was not miserable. I had cast off all feeling, subdued all anguish, to riot in the excess of my despair. Evil thenceforth

> became my good. Urged thus far, I had no choice
> but to adapt my nature to an element which I had
> willingly chosen. The completion of my demoniacal
> design became an insatiable passion. And now it is
> ended; there is my last victim! (217)

The monster was emotionally tied to his creator in such a way that they would never reach peace. He was a curse and nemesis of the sin committed. Born of passion unbound he became like his creator: "the slave...of an impulse which I detested yet could not disobey" (217). What Robert finds hovering over Victor, is his monster, created in his perfect image. A slave to insatiable passions that he once committed, he regrets with horror.

Conclusion

What began as the ambitions of a young man who "considered the improvement which every day takes place in science and mechanics" grew into "the birth of that passion, which afterwords ruled [his] destiny" (43, 26). Mary's Prometheus, unlike her husband's, discovers that there are natural grooves and ruts to the order of creation. There are consequences to unraveling the natural order: "Take but degree away, untune that string and hark what discord follows!"[14]

The world Mary Shelley made is a world in which a man came under the servitude of a wicked impulse that gave birth to a monster, and its consequences were sin, and ultimately, death. *Frankenstein* is a world where debts

---

14. William Shakespeare, *Troilus and Cressida*, Act 1, Scene 3.

unpaid are paid in full with the blood of the debtors. No other blood will do. There is no cross. There is no atonement. There is no salvation. Just you and the sum of your life's choices. And that is utterly terrifying.

In 1819 another of Mary's children died. Her biographer Miranda Seymour notes:

> In the summer of 1819, she could think of nothing but her loss. She had been a mother three times; each time, the child had been snatched from her. 'Oh, oh, oh how overwhelming you are,' Shelley had written, quoting Aeschylus, at the end of her first journal. What sin, she wondered, could have merited such relentless punishment? The old fashioned concept of divine retribution was not one Mary had learnt either from Godwin or Shelley; she began, nevertheless, to wonder if Harriet Shelley's death lay at her door and if this was the penalty that was exacted. The thought would linger, and haunt her.[15]

If anything is the basis for horror, it is that thought.

---

15. *Mary Shelley* (London: John Murray, 2000), 231.

21 SIGNIFICANT QUESTIONS & ANSWERS

1. How do the letter bookends aid the novel?

   The opening and closing letters provide the scope of the sandwiched story of Victor Frankenstein. An ambitious man (Walton) rescues a crazed man (Frankenstein) who offers ominous warnings. The crazed man offers his testimony in order that the ambitious man might repent of their shared madness.

2. How are Victor and Robert similar? How are they different?

   Upon hearing about Robert's hopes and dreams ("of acquiring knowledge which I sought, for the dominion he should acquire and transmit over the elemental foes of our race," p. 15), Victor's heart sinks. He hears the very same intemperate passion that brought about his ruin. Their difference is primarily

in relation to time, and is Robert's only hope. He has
the opportunity to turn back. He hasn't gone *too* far.

3.   Why does Victor tell Robert the story of his Creation?

In order for Robert to repent of his unbridled ambition for knowledge.

4.   In a story about creators and creatures, is there anything
of note about the relationship of Victor to his father?

One interesting aspect is Victor's father's disdain for
the kind of science that interests him most. Victor
draws a straight line to his father's seemingly igno-
rant hand wave of Agrippa as the thing that fueled
his interest. Had his father just taken the time to
thoroughly explain, "it is possible that the train of
my ideas would never have received the fatal impulse
that led to my ruin" (27). Similar to the monster's
relation towards him, he makes decisions in reaction
to his father that are fueled by emotional anxiety.
His reasoning and behavior are being steered by bit-
terness toward his progenitor.

5.   How does Victor describe the differences between the
science of Newton and the science of Agrippa?

The functional difference was the knowledge of or-
igin and final causes. "Sir Isaac Newton is said to
have avowed that he felt like a child picking up shells
beside the great and unexplored ocean of truth.... He
had partially unveiled the face of Nature, but her im-

mortal lineaments were still a wonder and a mystery. He might dissect, anatomize, and give names; but, not to speak of a final cause, causes in their secondary and tertiary grades were utterly unknown to him. I had gazed upon the fortifications and impediments that seemed to keep human beings from entering the citadel of nature, and rashly and ignorantly I had repined. But here were books, and here were men who had penetrated deeper and knew more. I took their word for all that they averred, and I became their disciple" (28).

6. What effect if any, does the death of his mother have on Victor?

> Victor's mother functions as his North Pole that tempers his passion. After her death he loses that, and his passions begin to lose regulation. He becomes a slave to his impulses.

7. What happens to the passion of Victor once his creation comes to life?

> The passion dissipates. All that is left once the monster opens his eyes is the horror of his project. He was blinded by his passion and false promises of what completion would gain him.

8. What is the significance of the books that the Monster mentions to Victor?

> The Monster has read *The Sorrows of Young Werther*, *Paradise Lost*, and *Plutarch's Lives*. Similar to his Creator, the reading of texts takes him to the highest of highs and lowest of lows emotionally. In reading *Paradise Lost* he identifies with Satan who, when he considers his creator, is riddled with envy. And with Werther he gleaned the imaginations and gloom of the main character and was filled with wonder at his suicide. *Plutarch's Lives* offers a model of virtue that he knows he should have but he can't achieve.

9. Why won't Victor be honest with friends and family about what he's done?

> Victor is ashamed. The existence of his Monster reveals previous motives of unhinged ambition. Additionally, those temptations lead to a sin with legs that haunts him and ultimately results in his death and the death of everyone he loves. In refusing to take responsibility, he grows more ashamed, and just runs away.

10. What is the monster's justification for murder?

> The monster confesses to being driven by an insatiable and horrible desire that he had no choice but to follow. He wanted what was not gifted to him, and he took it by any means necessary.

11. What is Victor's great sin in the novel?

> Untethered ambition that drives him to a breach of Nature, generating the Unnatural.

12. What important characteristics do we find in comparing the creature to his creator?

> Victor and his Monster are more alike than Victor would admit. Victor's monster is a carbon copy of himself. The supreme example is Victor tells us he lacks maturity emotionally. Passions take him wherever they will and don't let him go until it's too late. Similarly, the monster is at the will of his emotions. Unrequited wants drive him to insanity. He will gain what he lacks by any means necessary. And they both defend themselves with the same justification.

13. How does the death of Victor affect the Monster?

> Robert is surprised to see the Monster in pain and in deep regret. The envy the Monster has towards his creator binds him in ways that don't make sense to Robert. He oscillates between hatred and pity for his creator. He wants everything his creator has and if he can't have it, he'll take it from him. At the sight of his death, he is left without purpose, and heads to his funeral pyre.

14. In his final monologue, how does the Monster differentiate himself from Milton's Satan?

> The Monster references Milton's *Paradise Lost* again to differentiate himself from Satan to highlight his loneliness in his sin: "But it is even so; the fallen angel becomes a malignant devil. Yet even that enemy of God and man had friends and associates in his desolation; I am alone" (218).

15. Where does the Monster say he's headed when he leaves Robert's ship? Why?

> He tells Robert that he's headed for his funeral pyre, to kill himself. The person he loved most and hated the most has died, and it's his fault. Racked with pain and regret, only death can free him.

16. Victor told Robert his story in order that Robert would repent of his ambitions. Was he successful?

> Yes, Robert turns back.

17. How does knowing the life of the author help us understand the intentions behind *Frankenstein*?

> The life of the author clarifies questions that the text asks of the reader. What are we to do with a sentient monster with a romantic taste in books? What does Mary want us to think about the monster? It's clear that we are to heed the warnings of her Prometheus and not buy in to the lies of her husband.

18. How does the family in the Cottage function in relation to the rest of the story? What purpose do they serve for Mary's point?

> They are the romantic ideal, outside of society in harmony and happiness. This is the section of the book where our monster receives his romantic education. As Jean-Jacques Rousseau said, "Man is free but everywhere in chains," and this family is doing their best to live free. Mary also adds poverty to their list of characteristics which the monster reacts to in pity, offering us more than a grunting monster hungry for brains, but one that identifies and sympathizes with the suffering. Additionally, when the family runs him off given his hideous appearance, it puts more sympathetic hay in the barn for our creature.

19. Walton tells his sister Margaret that he will kill no albatross. What's the reference and how does it function in relation to the novel?

> The references are to Coleridge's poem, *The Rime of the Ancient Mariner*. In this poem a tale is recounted by an old mariner about a captain at sea near the Arctic that brings about death and bedlam when he shoots an Albatross. Walton uses it to what he's sure will be Margaret's joy: to indicate to her that he marvels and wonders at creation, thanks to the poets. He will commit no violence toward Nature. His safety should therefore be of no concern.

20. Is the monster a sympathetic creature?

> Answers may vary here. The creature is not a sympathetic character in the way director Guillermo Del Toro is quoted in this guide He demands the attention of his creator and will murder innocent people to gain it. Once he has the vengeful attention of his creator, he amplifies it by fleeing the country, egging on a chase. Once his creator has run himself to death in the chase, he decides to kill himself. In short, he was immaturely jealous for what he did not have, and was prepared to gain it any way he could.

21. Of all the people that the Monster killed, why did he only kill people who never even knew he existed?

> The Monster only destroys those that contribute security, happiness, and love to his Creator. He is not reacting to a lynch mob, out for blood with pitchforks and torches—killing in self-defense. Were that to be the case, Del Toro and critics like him might have grounds in their exalted sympathy. "For while I destroyed [Victor's] hopes, I did not satisfy my own desires" (218).

FURTHER DISCUSSION AND REVIEW

Master what you have read by reviewing and integrating the different elements of this classic.

SETTINGS AND CHARACTERS

Be able to compare and contrast the personalities (including strengths, weaknesses, and mannerisms) of each character. How does the setting affect characters?

PLOT

Be able to describe the beginning, middle, and end of the book along with specific details that move the plot forward and make it compelling. This includes the success or downfall (or both) of each character.

CONFLICT

Go through the character list and describe the tension between any and all main characters. Then, think about whether any characters have internal conflict (in their own minds). What is the purpose of the overt conflict (fighting), or any conflict with impersonal forces?

THEME STATEMENTS

Be able to describe what this classic is telling us about the world. Is the message true? What truth can we take from the plot, characters, conflict, and themes (even if the author didn't believe that truth)? Do any objects take on added meaning because of repetition or their place in the story (i.e., do any objects become symbols)? Be able to interact with and give examples for the following statements:

> God made the world in such a way that lawlessness and an abandonment of his moral law will create an insufferable and unhappy life.

> "But every man is tempted, when he is drawn away of his own lust, and enticed. Then when lust hath conceived, it bringeth forth sin: and sin, when it is finished, bringeth forth death." ~James 1:14-15

> The revolutionary spirit of the enlightenment presumed that institutions such as marriage enslaved its inhabitants, and casting it aside, they became slaves to their lust.

Finally, compose your own theme statement about some element, large or small, of this classic. Then use the Bible and common sense to assess the truth of that theme statement. Identify your own key words or borrow from the following list as a starting point: *Monster, Pity, Imagination, Ambition, Knowledge,* and *Love.*

A NOTE FROM THE PUBLISHER:
TAKING THE CLASSICS QUIZ

Once you have finished the worldview guide, you can prepare for the end-of-book test. Each test will consist of a short-answer section on the book itself and the author, a short-answer section on plot and the narrative, and a long-answer essay section on worldview, conflict, and themes.

Each quiz, along with other helps, can be downloaded for free at www.canonpress.com/ClassicsQuizzes. If you have any questions about the quiz or its answers or the Worldview Guides in general, you can contact Canon Press at service@canonpress.com or 208.892.8074.

ABOUT THE AUTHOR

Jake McAtee lives in Moscow, Idaho where he got his Master's at New Saint Andrews College. He works at Canon Press, and produces the Amazon Prime series *Man Rampant*. He is also the host of the *Canon Calls* podcast.

www.ingramcontent.com/pod-product-compliance
Lightning Source LLC
Chambersburg PA
CBHW071936020426
42331CB00010B/2890